PANIC

A PLAY IN VERSE

BOOKS BY ARCHIBALD MacLEISH

Archibald MacLeish

PANIC

A PLAY IN VERSE

BOSTON AND NEW YORK
HOUGHTON MIFFLIN COMPANY
The Riverside Press Cambridge
1935

Caution: Professionals and amateurs are hereby warned
that 'Panic,' being fully protected under the Copyright
Laws of the United States of America, is subject to
royalty.   All rights, including professional, amateur,
motion picture, recitation, public reading, radio broad-
casting, and the rights of translation into foreign lan-
guages are strictly reserved.   All inquiries regarding
this play should be addressed to the Phoenix Theatre,
Inc., 229 West 42nd Street, New York City.

The Riverside Press
CAMBRIDGE · MASSACHUSETTS
PRINTED IN THE U.S.A.

To JOHN *and* KATY DOS PASSOS

*Why should I explain to you that Those who are not
known have returned to us again? You also have seen them
from no chair in no window but suddenly as men learn
everything — as though the mind were, as it well may be, I
do not know, a swarm of invisible apprehensions which like
insects devour in silence and secretly the whole house: for it
falls in an instant's illumination and a collapse of darkness.*

A NOTE ON THE VERSE

ANY man who undertakes to write verse for the stage must face, sooner or later, a problem which is none the less fundamental because it is technical. He must attempt to find a verse form capable of catching and carrying the rhythm of the spoken language of his time and place. He will not be relieved of his obligation by the fact that the attempt may seem, both to himself and to others, presumptuous and ill-advised. The fact that men whose names are unapproachable finalities have made similar attempts, and successful attempts, before him does not mean that his problem also has been solved. For the problem of form in dramatic verse, though once solved and even greatly solved, was never yet solved once for all.

English blank verse is the great example. English blank verse as written by Marlowe and Shakespeare and Webster was, as nearly as any man can now judge, an admirable equivalent to the spoken language of the country and the period. But English blank verse, instead of solving the problem of the contemporary playwright, merely complicates it. So successful was blank verse in its time, so great is the prestige of the names associated with its use, that it has dominated the English speaking stage for three hundred years and all but killed the use of poetry in the theatre. For the plain fact of the matter is that Marlowe's mighty line, however appropriate to Elizabethan English, is not appropriate at all to twentieth-century American. It still remains great poetry. But as a vehicle for contemporary expression it is pure anachronism. To make a stage-American talk it is precisely comparable to clothing a stage-American in Walter Raleigh breeches and a billowy cloak.

The fact is obvious. The reason has not always been observed. The reason is that the rhythm of blank verse and the rhythms of the spoken language of our country are precisely opposed. The rhythm of blank verse is spacious, slow, noble, and elevated. It moves forward in muscular iambic march. Even when interrupted, even when passionate, blank verse is always marmoreal — an hysteria of statues. It is the poetic counterpart of a language — but of a language spoken in deliberate ages by violent and deliberate men: men ceremonial even in their hatreds, deliberate even in their laughter.

The rhythms of contemporary American speech on the other hand are nervous, not muscular; excited, not deliberate; vivid, not proud. To my ear — and a man can only testify after his own senses — the classical rhythm equivalent to American speech would be more nearly the trochee or the dactyl than the iamb of blank verse. The voices of men talking intently to each other in the offices or the mills or on the streets of this country *descend from* stressed syllables; they do not *rise toward* stressed syllables as do the voices of men speaking in Shakespeare's plays. But the words trochee and dactyl are confusing words. They refer to a prosody of syllables, a prosody which has never had any real relation to the genius of the English language and which has no relation whatever to the genius of the American language. The American language is a language of accents. Its most marked characteristic is its accentual strength — a strength which the more even, toneless, British tongue rarely achieves.

And its whole beauty and color, its great vigor and vitality, result from the sharpness and distinction of its stresses.

It is for this reason that blank verse is no solution of the American playwright's difficulties. And if blank verse is no solution, neither is a solution to be found in those relaxed forms of iambic composition which merely loosen the line until the tension essential to poetry disappears. The critic who tells a playwright that his verse is so free as to leave the audience doubtful whether it is prose or verse does not compliment him. Verse, after all, is not an arrangement upon the page: it is a pattern in the ear. If it does not exist in the ear, it does not exist.

The true solution would seem to me to be found in a very different direction — in the direction of a prosody frankly built upon accents without regard to syllabic interval. It is of course well known that English prosody, prior to the classic influence, was by nature non-syllabic and that it remained non-syllabic to a certain degree down to the date of Milton's verbal ceramics. And it is at least arguable, in spite of Chaucer and the Miltonic influence, that a true accentual poetry can again be written in English. If it can be, it will offer an instrument beautifully adapted to the representation in verse of the highly stressed vigorous speech of our time and country.

The verse of this play is an effort — certainly neither the first nor the last — in that direction. I have adopted for the principal scenes — scenes to be acted by bankers, radicals, lawyers — a line of five accents but unlimited syllables: the accent falling always in the position suggested by the sense. Some lines have as few as five syllables — all of them accented; others have as many as fifteen or seventeen syllables. But the pattern of five accents, five beats, is as regular as any convention in any form. Moreover, in almost all the lines of the play, the rhythm descends from strongly stressed first syllables to weak final syllables in a manner directly opposed to the manner of blank verse. For those who find the terminology of classical prosody helpful, the same thing may be said by saying that the rhythm is generally trochaic, sometimes dactyllic, sometimes spondaic. But it will, I hope, be difficult to reduce the verse to such elements over any length of time. What should appear is the regular pattern of five accents with a rhythm falling away from the tension of the stress.

In those sections to be spoken by voices in a street crowd, I have varied the form by using a three-beat line constructed like the five-beat line of the body of the poem. The only major difference is that the verse of the street scenes is written for the most part in couplets linked by assonance.

Of the construction of the play as a whole it is only necessary to remark that the attempt to use the crowd as an actor has resulted in a chorus speaking, not with the single voice of the Greek chorus, but with the many voices of the American street.

A. MacL.

Conway
November 1934

PANIC

A PLAY IN VERSE

PERSONS OF THE PLAY

McGAFFERTY — *owner of the country's principal industries and greatest bank; the leading industrialist and financier of his time. A man in his late fifties.*

IONE — *his mistress. A woman of thirty.*

IMMELMAN — *president of McGafferty's bank. Middle-aged.*

GRIGGS — *a steel company lawyer. McGafferty's age or older.*

A group of Bankers.

A delegation of Unemployed.

Two Bank Guards.

A Street Crowd: men, women, some well-dressed, some miserably — people of all kinds and classes.

SCENE

The action takes place in McGafferty's Office *in New York and in a street before an electric news bulletin of the Times Square type — moving words in lighted letters. Both are represented upon the same stage without division between them: the street upon the apron of the stage with the news bulletin hidden by the proscenium arch above it and visible to the audience only by the moving blurs of light; the office behind. The office, raised by several steps and enclosed on the sides by open square columns, at the back by a double door, consists of a long table, chairs, a news ticker. The whole scene is impersonal, bare, huge — on a scale to dwarf the shapes of men and women.*

TIME

Five-thirty to past seven of an evening in late February, 1933.

As the curtain rises The Street *is faintly lighted by the jerking flashes of the bulletin. There are a few men and women before it, their raised faces caught by the light. A few more approach. They speak not to each other but as though alone. Words read from the bulletin (printed in italics) are spoken at a regular lagging beat as the machine forms them.*

CONFUSED VOICES

Foreclosures in...

closed...

foreclosing...

Factories   closing   doors...

Billions   in balances   frozen...

3

Doors   closing...   foreclosed...

A WOMAN

Closing as doors close with
Death in a woman's house when the
Wind closes them.

A MAN

Thousands
Silent at closed doors.

A MAN

Silent: the doors closing: the
Life stopped.

A WOMAN

Comes over us
Slowly with closing of doors: with
Lights put out: with the stoves
Cold: the hands numb.

AN OLD MAN

Slowly the thing comes.
There are many signs: there are furnaces
Dead now that were burning
Thirty years in a town —
Never dark: there are foundries —

4

Fires drawn: trestles
Silent. The swifts nest in
Stacks that for generations
Flowed smoke. The patience of
Hawks is over the cities:
They circle in clean light where the
Smoke last year frightened them.

A WOMAN

The gears turn: twitter: are
Still now. The sound dies.
From the east with the sun's rising
Daily are fewer whistles:
Many mornings listening
One less or two.

A YOUNG MAN

The thing comes pursuing us
Creeping as death creeps in an
Old man: as sleep comes:
Leaving on one hill —
On the stand — the stalks silver —
Corn rotted in ear:
Leaving on land nearest us
Wagons abandoned: milk cows
Slaughtered for no sickness:
Rigs rusting at pit-heads:
Pumps frozen: switches

Green with the rain: the oil
Thickened: scale in boilers —
Good gear all of it:
Sound metal: faultless:
Idle now: never manned.

A GIRL

Men in the dusk — and they stand there
Letting the girls go by with the
Sweet scent: silent:
Leaning heavily: bent to the
Painted signs on the fences —
They that in other times
Calling after us climbed by the
Steep stair for the sight of a
Girl's knee delighting her.

A MAN

From what ill and what enemy
Armless shall we defend the
Evening — the night hours?

A MAN

No eyes of ours have
Ever knowing beheld it.
It comes not with the bells
Arousing towns: racing with
Smoke — with the wind's haste —
The tallest houses toppled.

6

A MAN

Comes not from the hospitals —
Odor of scattered lime —
Night burials climbing the
Empty streets by the markets.

A MAN

Not with the shot: with the barking of
Dogs before color of dawn —
The whistle over the lawn — the
Running footfall stumbling.

A WOMAN

Nevertheless it comes.
Men die: houses
Fall among kitchen flowers.
Families scatter. Children
Wander the roads building of
Broken boxes shelter.
A land of great wealth and the
Old hungry: the young
Starving — but not with hunger.
None have beheld this enemy.
What arms can defend the
Evening — the night hours —
When fear: faceless: devours us?

A Woman

Blight — not on the grain!
Drouth — not in the springs!
Rot — not from the rain!

A Man

What shadow hidden or
Unseen hand in our midst
Ceaselessly touches our faces?

The light of the bulletin flickers out: the street vanishes: the light comes on in McGafferty's Office: *a strong, clear, white light — the whole scene in sharp profile of black upon white. McGafferty sits at the head of the long table facing the audience. He is a strongly built man, his face florid, his hair barely grey, his gestures decisive. Around the table on straight chairs sit the Bankers, rigid in their short black jackets and piped trousers (London model). They move and gesture together but not with a mechanical precision. Beside the table at the edge of the light Immelman, the type of hollow, brittle, socially correct banker, leans over the news ticker. The sound of the instrument (sometimes the whir of the mechanism: sometimes the beat of the type) comes in intervals of sound over intervals of silence: a rhythm parallel to the rhythm of the verse. The Bankers speak in rotation — first one and then the next. They are eight or ten in number. As Immelman speaks they turn toward the ticker.*

Immelman (reading)

Atlanta... Seaman's National... branch closed.
Indianapolis... People's and Guaranty... closes.
Frankfort... Farm Mortgage... forced closing.
Memphis... Mechanics closed... National closing.
Louisville... Lincoln Title & Loan... closed —

8

McGafferty

Yes and twenty more. And why? What's done it?
Who's behind it? That's the question gentlemen.
Things like this don't happen by themselves.
What's behind it? Who is?

The Bankers swing toward McGafferty turning in their chairs.

The Bankers
What's behind it!

Who knows what's behind it?

Who can tell us?

Ask the economists! Ask the professors — the best of them!

Ask the man in the plowed lot — the farmer:
The owners of famous wells: successful merchants:
Men accustomed to great risks at sea:
Drovers out of the Southwest with the guns on them:
Silver miners: Iowa pig-feeders: railroaders —
Builders of line and the sons of the builders of line!

Ask the fishermen fast to their winter cables —
Mackerel making the bays boil — and afraid —
All afraid — and of what? For God's sake fearing
What with their haltered ships and their cancelled orders?
They don't know it to tell. They've never seen it.

9

What do they know of it? Nothing. And three years:
Each year worse than last year. Now there's this one.

McGAFFERTY

Don't tell me it's blind. I know it's blind.
We're here because it's blind. It's not that blind though.
Best bank closes sometime: strongest falter:
Men can die that never died before.
It's not that blind. There's nothing secret — mysterious:
Nothing men with human brains can't handle.
Smoke's a sign of fire: we can find it.

IMMELMAN (*reading*)

Michigan... Guardian Trust... loans called.

The Bankers swing toward the ticker: rise: swing back toward McGafferty.

THE BANKERS

Smoke!

Smoke on the wind!

Smoke of a brush fire!

Smoke of a blaze in the brush and the rush of the wind in it!

Ever go out with the smoke in your mouth McGafferty?

10

Ever watch it McGafferty running in pine-land?

Ever watch how the pines go up in a big one —
Exploding like shells — ten together or twenty or
One on a hill in a white flash and the burst of it
Bumping the smoke open?

Great sight McGafferty!
Great sight on a dry day — to be wondering
When she'll go and whether she'll go and what started it!

Nobody knowing what started it!

Nobody knowing!

McGAFFERTY (*rising*)
No? Well I will gentlemen: I'll learn it —

IMMELMAN (*reading*)
Michigan... Governor called... crowds threatening.

The Bankers push forward toward McGafferty.

THE BANKERS
Easy enough for you McGafferty riding the
World with your great bank and your great fortune —
People speaking your name with wonder!

11

Governments
Begging their bread from you! Easy enough for you!

Easy enough for you with the cash and the credits to
Rattle the roost with your crowing but what of the rest of us —
Barely the brass in the box for a day's call and the
Fat fools in the lines with their frozen faces
Chucking their check books at the teller's cage?

What about us?

What of the rest of us?

Question! —
Christ! We know the question! What's the answer?

Nobody guessing the answer!

Economics!
Used to fight in the open with live men —
James J. Hill and the Wars of the Burlington.
Those days were easy to these days.

No one against you... boat in a fog... motionless...
Bell away off and a bell and another...
Sound shifting with each sea till you're lost to it.
How can you fight fog? How can you fight it?

Blind — all blind — like a scrap in an alley.

12

Something there you can't see but it's there:
You can't hear it even. You can't lay hands on it.

Kind of plague of the soul a man might say!
Every need to live by and they won't live.
Old days there were plagues of the flesh — famine:
Bad crops: pestilence: things you could see.
Now there's nothing — good health — fat land — bins full.
Yes — and still they're sick of it: still dying.

McGafferty

God you talk like girls that see a ghost!
There's only men and weather in this world: —
The rest is wishing. You can stand and fight or
Run and not fight but your choice will choose it.

*The Bankers recoil. As they speak they retreat across the room
drawing together.*

The Bankers

What can we fight?

What can we see?

What can we

See to fight?

Nothing to fight against.

13

                                        No one — there's
No one. There's nothing.

                        Fighting the fog.

                                    Fighting the
Fall of the night and there's nothing.

                            No one against us:
No one!

                The dead stacks: the black dust: the
Rust on the tracks and there's no one.

                          The silence in valleys.

The factories lightless at dusk by the sidings: the couplings
Loose in the yards and no one: there's nothing.

                                Riders on
Rods and on roads and by water and running away and from
No one: the loads in the Fords and from far and from no one.

Running away from it.

                      Silence in valleys: the railways — the
Weeds on the slag and the goldenrod rank on the switch-iron.

Silence: the freights on the grade light and not often: the
Long whistle at night for the crossing and silence.
The lanterns unlighted in barns nor the barking of dogs by them.

IMMELMAN

Guardian gone in Detroit! Guardian closing!

The Bankers wheel toward the ticker.

THE BANKERS

Guardian

God! if the Guardian...

Guardian closing!

Guardian closing — that settles it: sinks it!

The Guardian!

McGAFFERTY (*to* IMMELMAN)

Sure of it?

IMMELMAN

Says so. The Guardian. Doors closed.
Word's on the wire now. News breaking.

15

The Bankers move away from the ticker. The light of the office begins slowly to dim out. The street crowd is seen moving darkly beside the office and below it. The sound of the ticker grows louder.

THE BANKERS

News breaking! God in Heaven!

Panic!

Women awakened! Feet running!

Newspapers! —
Extras at late night — men shouting:
Not boys!

Shouting! Hoarser voices!
Windows opened!

Lights lit!

Wakening city!

The light in McGafferty's Office is out. The pulsing flash of the bulletin board begins in The Street *— the flashes picking up the staccato rhythm of the Bankers' voices. The first glimpses of light show the Street almost empty — a few faces lifted to the board. As*

16

the flashes continue men and women come quickly toward the light speaking as they come.

VOICES IN THE STREET

What's it about?

What is it

Saying?

What about banks is it?

What about banks? Is it runs on the
Banks is it?

What does it say?

What about runs on the banks is it
Saying?

What about banks?

Is it

Runs on the banks is it? Christ! is it
Runs on the banks?

On the banks.

A MAN (*reading*)

| *Thousands in* | *throngs.* | *Thanks us for* |
| *Keeping* | *calm* | *in the Crisis.* |

17

A Woman

Why is it happening? Why is it?

A Man

Price of a woolen blanket!
Price of a decent bed!

A Woman

After it all: after everything!

A Woman

Our Father who art Thou in Heaven
Forgive us our daily bread!

A Man

Keeping calm in the crisis!

A Woman

Keeping with downcast eyes
In dark streets at daybreak
Frightened files: laborers:
Foreign women: they shuffle
Onward little enough
Clutching at bank-book papers.

A Woman

Onward as those that escape in
Dreams the seeming pursuers —

Fleeing they only move by
Inching steps: stumblingly!

A Woman

Silent: their eyes humble:
The meek umbrellas over them.

An Old Man

A man's savings pared from the
Heel of every loaf —
He hungry: sparing the
Smallest mouthful: purchasing
Old age painfully —
Fear of death urges him.

A Young Man

To be frightened — to fear death — is
Nothing: is man's lot: is
Many ages' wisdom!
Fear of hunger is misery!

A Man

Fear of sickness — abandoned!

A Man

Mute in motionless panic
Many at street corners
Stand staring before them:

19

Spitting: speaking little:
Fearing a greater ill.

A Woman
Father who art Thou in...

A Man
                           Thanks us for
Keeping calm in the crisis!

An Old Woman
Surely a curse lies on us!
No common evil!
No!... the luck leaves us!

An Old Man
The good man in his chair: the
Child at its play will perish — by
What hand ignorant —
Either for what sin —
Whether his own or another's or
Everyman's — or for nothing:
Whether by God's blow or
God's blindness!

An Old Man
            Knowing
Never for what fault or

Failing of ours is altered the
World's future suddenly —
Spilling of what blood:
Thing done or not done:
Holy duty forgotten —
Knowing neither the fault nor the
Finder — nevertheless
We know well His messenger!
Death we have always known!

A WOMAN

Where the eyes of death are
Shown are shown against us
Signals of God's enmity!

A WOMAN

We have beheld them — thousands —
Dead man in blameless house!

MEN'S VOICES (*reading*)

Bankers   summoned to   conference.

Mister   McGafferty   summons...

Government   calls on   McGafferty.

A MAN

McGafferty!

21

A WOMAN

McGafferty helping us!

A WOMAN

McGafferty! Hope still!

A MAN

He helping is hope!

A WOMAN

A great man! A brave one!

A MAN

McGafferty! Help-hand! One left!

A WOMAN

None but he helpful!

A WOMAN

In him hope — in McGafferty!

The light of the Street fades out. The light of The Office *comes on as before. The Bankers are crowded around McGafferty: McGafferty seated. The sound of the ticker is more noticeable: the tempo faster. Immelman still stands beside it.*

THE BANKERS

What shall we do McGafferty?

What shall we do?

What about you McGafferty?

                              What are you going to
Do McGafferty?

                         What about you — what will you
Do now?

McGafferty

Do? What do you think I'll do?
Pull the blinds on the bank and sail for Bermuda?
This bank will open tomorrow at nine and
Open thereafter at nine and open thereafter at
Nine o'clock for a long spell: maybe longer!
Might stay open a year — you can't tell!
Might be a wall or a roof or a weathervane standing a
Couple of years from now: or even three: or a
Brass plaque in its place on the site of the post office!
Better come back for a look! You'll find me waiting!

Immelman (*reading*)

Files camped in the street at the Bowery Savings.

*McGafferty swings violently to his feet. The Bankers recoil. As
McGafferty speaks, a confused and rising noise of voices is heard
beyond the door. The Bankers retreat to the far end of the table.*

McGafferty

What for God's sake did you think I'd do?
What *can* we do but face it — raise the cash —

23

Carry the wrecked ones till the wind blows over?
They'll sink us with them if we don't. Look here —
A hundred million's easy round this table.
A hundred million does it — stops the runs —
Flattens the fear out. It's been done before.
Our fathers did it.

The noise increases.

These things pass.

The noise increases: blows at the door.

The wind falls...

*The noise suddenly rises drowning out McGafferty's voice. The
doors are thrown open. Two Bank Guards in grey uniforms are
forced back into the doorway by a small mob of ten or twelve — all
young, all bareheaded, all in leather jackets: one of them blind with
a white ecstatic face. Like the Bankers they move and gesture roughly
together: speak one after the other in rotation. They look in over the
straining shoulders of the Guards.*

A GUARD

Move! Move can't you! God damned Radicals!
Get your shoes on their shins O'Connell to shatter them!

THE UNEMPLOYED

There they are!

That's them!

24

The Bloodsuckers!

What do you think of it now Bloodsuckers?

Look at them!

What do you think of your world now Bloodsuckers?

A GUARD

Come on! Come on! Get out of it!

THE UNEMPLOYED

Anyone tell you what's happening Captains of Industry?

Anyone tell you the word for it?

What do you think —
What do you think would be happening Empire Builders?

Why should she crack with the banks rich and the factories
Rolling 'em out by the millions: radios everywhere:
Dynamos bigger than God: vacuum cleaners in
Four flats out of three and the furnace electric —

Think it's an accident Captains? Didn't they tell you?

Didn't you know it was coming? Didn't they tell?

Didn't you know it was this that was coming Captains?

A Guard

That's enough! That's enough of it! Quiet now!

The Unemployed

Ever study the histories Empire Builders?
Ever read in the books how your world would run?
Runs like a hare in a hunt: you can name the circle!
Runs in a groove with the crack of a gun at the end of it!

Blood on the wall at the end of it!

Us at the end of it!

Our world at the end: a new world!

Didn't you know it was us would come after you Captains?

Nothing in all your Hells can stop it now.

Nothing can help you now Captains. It's our world!
History's back of us! Time's bearing us! Life is a
Full flood in our hearts and in yours hollow!

The Guards

Brushed in like brats Mr. McGafferty!

Come by the back somehow: storming the corridors!

One blind in the eye what's worse to strike.

26

McGafferty

You'll stand back and let them come in the two of you!
Stand back I say! Take your arms down!

The Bankers retreat sharply to the farthest limits of the light. They stand pressed against each other in a solid group. McGafferty who has stood motionless reseats himself at the end of the table leaning back in his chair. The Blind Man stands between the Guards. The Unemployed behind him surge forward: fill the door: stop.

The Bankers (*rapidly*)

McGafferty I protest...

Preposterous!...

Impossible!...

Dangerous men!...

Outrageous!...

Damnable outrage!...

McGafferty

There you are gentlemen! There's your ghost!
There's a shadow to fear if you want shadows!
There's a nigger for your haunted wood-pile!
Maybe it's these boys did it! All! With jack-knives!
Maybe it's these you feared and never knew it
Better get back to your banks and mount the machine guns!
Better be writing the newspapers gentlemen warning them!

27

*The Blind Man moves forward into the room searching for McGaf-
ferty with his closed eyes.*

The Blind Man

Is that the man? Is that him? McGafferty?

McGafferty

There's the thing to scare you — boys like those! —
Feeble: underfed: tubercular: crippled:
Crazy with hatred as a dog with ticks!
There's the thing to scare you! Better drop it!
Better give in to them now while you still can!

*McGafferty swings his head toward the boys in the door: they retreat
a step.*

There's your nightmare! All your nightmares! All of them!
Things you see and don't see!

The Bankers (*rapidly*)
Scolded like schoolboys...

Can't be talked to like...

Serious conference...

... crisis!

The Blind Man

He's right. He's always right. You need not fear us!
And there are millions more you need not fear —
Feeble as we are: sick as we are: hungry:

28

Torpid with hunger: tiring to be dead —
The torpor of death: the horrible dying of apathy!
Men who dread to sleep lest dreams deceive them!
The hopeless — having lost the wish to hope!
The men with folded hands! You need not fear them!
Tongues harangue them but you need not fear!
Mouths incite them to fight and they will not answer!
Women hold them their wilted tits in contempt and they
Look down: they are dumb! You need not fear them!
Greatness they have forgotten and pride and the envy of
Nobler lives than their own and the service of honor.
To suffer for no gain: to invite death in the
Hope only of good is a fool's fate to them.
The man they praise is the man who has gotten away with it —
The slave with the wise slave's tricks — the cleverest victim.
Virtue and nobleness: honor and love they laugh at!...
Their speech is irony: the whipped man's speech:
They've lived a long life in the world you made them.
They've learned well in your world. You need not fear.

The Bankers move forward a step.

THE BANKERS (*rapidly*)
Haven't we anything better to do than listen to
Wild talk with the...

Soap box speeches...

Radicals...

Billions in balance and...

... Better to do than listen to...

The Blind Man

It is not we you have the need to fear —
Our eyes are blind: our broken fingers crippled.
It is not we should break your sleep at night.
We are your body — sick that you may perish!
We are your anguish — paid that you may perish!
We are your Christ — your million Christs — who writhe: but
Not that you may live — that you may perish!

A Guard

Quiet I tell you! Quiet! Somebody handle him!

The Blind Man

It is not we you have the need to fear!
No! But when the day comes — when the day is
Come — when that day comes to you — on that day —
Needless and nameless though the fear may be — you'll
Learn the taste of it. You'll see our hunger —
Yes! And that day you will fear our hunger!
Cold you'll see us and you'll fear our cold!
Sick — sick till the blood turns — and you'll fear us!
That day you will see us and the sight will
Frighten you! It is not we who kill...

30

THE BANKERS

For God's sake McGafferty!

Call him off!

THE BLIND MAN

... It is not we who threaten you! Your ill is
Time and there's no cure for time but dying!

THE BANKERS

That's enough McGafferty!

Choke him can't you?

THE BLIND MAN

Time's the hurt your hearts have: not our hands.
Your fate is yours but written in our hatred —
Read in our anguish — shrieking from our graves.
Your destiny is yours but our arms' burden.

THE BANKERS

I'm going: who else?

I am!

I am!

I am!

That's enough of it for one day!

I am!

31

The Bankers wheel toward the door: face the Blind Man: stop.

MCGAFFERTY

Ask him when the world ends gentlemen.
Ask him for the date of doom. He'll tell you.

*The Blind Man turns sharply toward McGafferty's voice: groping:
his hands out. Speaking he moves toward him.*

THE BLIND MAN

Yes...

    He'll tell you...

        And you'll hear him...

            Listen!

Listen McGafferty! The day will come!
This time or the next time — now or after —
One crash or the certain crash beyond!
You'll sleep between them and forget — but we won't.
Once the need has left you you'll forget.
Men forget in good years with the grass green.
Men will say 'That's done now' — but it's not done:
Say 'That's over' — It will not be over:
Say 'What fools we were to fear it.' Fools! —
But not to fear it: to forget to fear!

32

McGAFFERTY (*rising from his chair*)

That's it gentlemen! That turns your cheeks white!
Schoolboys writing bloody words on fences!
Children with chalk!

THE BLIND MAN (*moving always toward McGafferty — his
hands out*)

The prophecies come true
Not of themselves but of the ears that hear them.
The violence works in the blood. The living inherit the
Hard speech of the dead like the seed of a pestilence.
They carry it close in their mouths and their breath feeds it.
You yourselves will feed it and will die.
You yourselves in your own minds will make the
Fate that murders you. The bursting seed of
Death is rotting ripe beneath your tongues!

*The Blind Man's groping fingers touch McGafferty's sleeve: rise:
move on his shoulders: touch his face. There is no sound but the
drumlike beat of the ticker, slow and insistent. The Unemployed
in the door and the Bankers across the room move forward a step.
McGafferty does not stir. Suddenly the Blind Man's hands fall:
he steps back: his arms held out rigidly from his sides.*

McGAFFERTY

No more prophecies? The chalk not working?

*The Blind Man steps back again: the Unemployed and the Bankers
forward.*

McGAFFERTY

All the bloody words gone?

33

*The Blind Man lets his hands fall to his sides. He speaks gently –
almost with tenderness. His voice low.*

THE BLIND MAN

(Against fate
Even the strongest have not overcome.)
As water pursues on the grooved earth its channel
Choosing without choice so man his fortune —
Choosing without choice. Yours is disaster.
The will is made in your own mind to die.
Even in rich land: the loam deep:
The wheat covering earth: the roaring of forests
Following mountain to mountain the southwest wind
(You doubt not in your heart doom is your destiny.
(Neither the annual rings of the oaks nor the records of
Rain comfort you reading in your own heart.
Not by the year's dearth or the earth's yield is
Man's fortune deciphered or fate told.
Field of the earth was never to fate fallow —
Only in furrows of men's minds are sown the
Seeds that ripening are destiny.)
You yourself — desiring your own death —
Neither wealth nor richness of earth nor turning of
Wheels perfectly under the acre roofs nor the
Proud piling of ingots prevails over the
Mute will in your mind to suffer destruction.
(No power of force or of violence can weaken the
Willingness in your own mind to die.)

34

With the last words the light has faded out in the Office: the ticker continues in the dark: dies. The light comes on again in The Street *where a few men and women stand before the Board.*

A MAN

Radicals   heckle   McGafferty.

A MAN

Radicals!

A MAN

Swinging the haft of the
Big axe aint they?

A MAN

Greatest   banker   baited.

A MAN

Him baited? McGafferty?

A MAN

Fall   of leader   foretold.

A WOMAN

Fall? McGafferty falling?

A WOMAN

That man also!

35

A Man

Sure! With the mountains!

A Man

McGafferty!

Him is it? When do we laugh?

A Man

Whose fall? McGafferty's?
After the rest of them! After the
Last of the rest and a long time!

A Woman

Not many as strong!

A Woman

Nor any of more wealth in the
World's time as they tell us —
Even Jews! And the women
Wishing only for him —
Thinking the cars they'd have with the
Soft seats and the Avenue
Blue with moon: and the flowers —
A rich man and a powerful!
Who will be overthrowing a
Man like him with a blow?

36

A MAN

Overthrowing McGafferty!
Even fools would have laughed at it!

A MAN

Name known in the foreign
Mountains: spoken in wars:
Spoken in all men's tongues —
Like the words for salt and for hunger!

A MAN

Spoken by signs and among the
Nakedest men and in cities and
Over the water pits in the
Wild plains and at fords:
At the camel halts on the borders!

A MAN

Over the zinc bars and
Over the glass!

A MAN

    And in harbors and
Far at sea — the stokers
Clanging the coal in!

A MAN

    Spoken by
Mouths: stamped on the steel —

Lettered on ocean keels on the
Cold plates — the water
Washing the weeds on it!

A Man

                                          Taught from the
Grip of a gang boss' gun to the
Niggers naked in sunlight!

A Man

Dug out of wounds — splinters of
Shrapnel showing it!

A Man

                                          Printed on
Fifty gallon cans on the
Saddled mules by the shanties!

A Man

Overthrowing McGafferty!
Overthrowing the half of the
Common world — if they could!

A Man

Destiny dooms him it says!

A Man

You know! Signs in the west!
Star falls!

A Man

The three bitches with
One eye and the hitch of the
Woolen thread on their thumbs and the
Scissors for what's to become of us!

A Man

Bringing him down! Destiny!
That one!

An Old Woman

Nevertheless it's an
Ill name to be light with!
Which of us knows the why or the
When or the where either of
What's moving beneath in the
Trouble of times? It might be
Men in the past were right and
Fate does drive us! Covered with
Gable of God's love in the
Years when the church was standing we
Slept in peace in the land.
If there were stars they were hid from us.
Now that the roof's riddled we
See again! Stars march and the
Mute indifferent dark has
Purposes not for us but
Touching us! — turn as we must! —

Die as we can! There's something
Stronger than we that comes with the
Starved — the darkened fires:
Some power desiring
Harm to us all: and to him too.

A Man

Talk for the old women!

A Man

Talk for a fool! Destiny! —
Best three out of two and the
Winner take everything! *You* know!
All of us know! They've shown us the
Shape of it often enough!

A Man

The great McGafferty suffering
Fate's envy in silence! —
A likely thing!

The Old Woman
                Silent or
Not silent — suffering!

A Man

Not him! A tough one! A
Man of wealth in the world!

40

The light fades out in The Street: *comes on again in* McGafferty's
Office. *The Unemployed and the Guards are gone — the doors still
standing open. The Bankers, crowded together, move back toward the
door. Immelman is still at the ticker: its beat comes excitedly —
rapidly.*

THE BANKERS

Count us out!

Count the National out!

Fidelity Trust is out!

We're out — Fechtheim's!

MCGAFFERTY

All right! All right gentlemen!
Make it an even fifty. I'll take fifty.
Call it five apiece for you. It's nothing.
Fifty million's nothing...

IMMELMAN

Riots in Delaware.
Mine explosion in Utah. Factory fired.
Laying them off in Buffalo — seven thousand.

The Bankers edge toward the door.

A BANKER

Count the lot of us out!

41

MCGAFFERTY

Five million:
Five million dollars to stop it! I tell you
You can't quit! You can't do it!

The Bankers push into the doorway.

THE BANKERS

Can't we!

Watch us then!

Who says we can't?

Why can't we?

Every man for himself in a sea McGafferty!

Every man for his own roof in a flood!

Every man for himself and to Hell with the rest of them!

The Bankers back through the door.

MCGAFFERTY

Do as you like! Do as you like and be damned!
Close your false-front banks and hide the assets!
Hand the coin to your wives and the stock to your daughters!

42

Default your bonds and keep the cash for bail!
Cover your tracks! Save your skins! Run for it!
Where will you run? for the Isles of Greece? like Byron? — but
Not quite? Friends of Greece and of Freedom!
God you're a beautiful sight to see with the fright in your
Wet eyes and the fat in your belts and the fear on you!

The Bankers have gone. McGafferty stands for a moment staring after them.

McGafferty

Do as you like! I'll stay! I'll stay and fight it!
Christ I'll fight it! *One* will! I'll be standing!

There is a silence filled by the hurrying rattle of the ticker. McGafferty drops back into his chair: sits staring ahead.

Immelman

San Francisco: San Diego: Los Angeles...
Mobs forming in Fargo: mills bombed...

There is a moment's silence: the ticker clamorous: McGafferty not moving: Immelman motionless.

McGafferty

Who rigged it Immelman?

43

IMMELMAN

Who rigged what? — in Fargo?
Mess in California? I don't know.

McGAFFERTY

Not in California.

IMMELMAN

I don't get you.

McGAFFERTY

Try to get me.

IMMELMAN

Not in California?

McGAFFERTY

Ever hear of half a dozen hoodlums
Raiding the board room of a full-size bank?

IMMELMAN

Meaning what?

McGAFFERTY

You tell me what I mean!

44

Immelman straightens: turns: walks two steps toward McGafferty.
McGafferty still stares ahead.

IMMELMAN

You mean I had a hand?...

McGAFFERTY

           A hand? I don't know.
Ears! You've got your ears. Some bastard did it.
Which? You tell me. Which bright financier
Thought he'd bluff us with a mob of bums to
Back off — back down? Which one?

IMMELMAN

                  None I know of.

McGAFFERTY

No! You wouldn't know! Who runs this business?
You do don't you? Run the whole damn bank!
Tell me Mondays what you please to tell me!
No! You wouldn't know!

IMMELMAN

             They wouldn't do it.
There's none of them would do a thing like that.
They wouldn't dare to. None of them would dare.

McGAFFERTY

They wouldn't? And who would?

45

IMMELMAN

I don't know: no one.

McGAFFERTY

The bums just came: is that it?

IMMELMAN

Well — they came.

McGAFFERTY

You mean God sent them.

IMMELMAN

Really Mr. McGafferty...

McGAFFERTY

Showed them McGafferty as in a dream —
Broke and his pockets full of sand to sink with:
Sent them to bring the tidings up?

IMMELMAN

But really...

McGAFFERTY

Maybe you see me on the street yourself?
Maybe I'll soon be there and you can see me?

IMMELMAN

O for God's sake!

46

McGAFFERTY

You can't see? He saw it.
Touched me with tiny finger tips that saw it.
Nobody told him what to see. He saw it.

IMMELMAN

Nobody told him anything.

McGAFFERTY

I hear you.
Nobody told him. Saw it all himself.
The boy's another Jesus! Foresees death —
Foresees disaster! You stiff blundering fool!
Am I that old? Senile already? Doddering?

McGafferty swings around the table toward Immelman.

McGAFFERTY

Tell me which one did it Immelman!

IMMELMAN

I tell you they just came: they came: they broke in.

McGAFFERTY

Tell me which one did it! Who's against me?
God I'd break him for it if I knew!
Some man's hand's against me in it: whose is?

47

IMMELMAN

No one. There was no one.

McGAFFERTY

They just came!
You told me: they just came! It's *them* against us.
That's your story? It's the Revolution!
That's your story is it? Jesus Christ!
The Revolution!

McGafferty turns and walks back and forth behind the table.

McGAFFERTY

That kind!
The sick souls
Herding like hogs in the hang of the dark to be rid of the
Man's burden of living their forefathers won for them! —
Rid of the liberty! — rid of the hard choice! —
The free man's choosing of the free man's journey!
Running as lost hogs run — from the fear of their loneliness:
Hunting for one thing only — for the herd —
For the smell of the herd boar's rump against their noses — the
Reek of the rest: a safe life without dignity:
Death in the comfort of each other's dung:
Safe from themselves: safe from the risk and the run of their
Own lives. The Revolution — the nunnery!
What can men like that destroy or injure?
What can they do? What's to fear in them?

48

IMMELMAN

There's no one we should fear. There's no one did it...

McGAFFERTY

Calling it love of humanity! Love of humanity!
What's the love of humanity? Hatred of manhood!
Hatred of one man: love of men by hundreds!
Love of what's least like a man: unliving:
Nameless: faceless: sexless: odorless: blank:
Without breath: unreal: made of words: of numbers —
Love as prudes love: love in books: on paper —
Love! Not love but envy — but revenge —
But fear: hatred of life: horror of manhood!
Men who love humanity are men who
Hate the man: who'd first destroy him: that kind!
Their kind shrieking at us!

IMMELMAN (*abstractedly: the tape in his fingers*)
I know... I know...

McGAFFERTY

History's back of them! Fate's in their laps! And who says so?
Who ties this tin can to the live dog's tail and
Tells him it's the law no dog escapes from?
Who knows so much? Who makes the past our master?
History's the father-land to those who
Have none: for the rest — who have — a grave!

49

IMMELMAN (*watching McGafferty*)

We'd face it standing with the loans in. Say we
Called them! Say...

MCGAFFERTY

What makes their hearts so sure?
Who told them? How can they know? Who'll destroy us?
Christ it's always one man makes a world: —
One man called Magellan: called Lenin:
Called Cromwell: Rothschild: Leonardo:
One man making one man's bed to sleep in:
Making his bed in the brown water — De Soto —
The trees float on it: making on foreign streets in the
Dangerous cities his cold bed: exiled:
Cancer eating him: running his own risk:
Raising his face in the sun...

IMMELMAN

If we should call them...
Hell may break in half before tomorrow!
Let me call them now — before tomorrow!
Let me call them —

MCGAFFERTY (*turning on him*)

Call what?

IMMELMAN

Get the loans in.

McGAFFERTY

This bank call its loans?

IMMELMAN

If we should need them...

McGAFFERTY

This bank? Are you drunk? You'd knock the country
Clean through the crack of panic if you did!
No by God! We'll stay with it! We'll stop it!

IMMELMAN

Stop it! How?

McGAFFERTY

How *would* you stop it? Credit.

IMMELMAN

How? The pool won't back us.

McGAFFERTY

Then with no pool.

IMMELMAN

How with no pool?

McGAFFERTY

Paper man! With paper!
Call Chicago. Have him draw for fifty.

51

Draw on him for fifty. Kite the checks.
Load the banks that need it. Keep them kited.
Three days ought to see us through!

IMMELMAN

                                        Chicago!
Chicago's overdrawn with us since noon.

McGAFFERTY

To Hell with that. We'll think of that tomorrow.
Call him!

IMMELMAN

              No but...

McGAFFERTY

              Get the call in.

*Immelman crosses slowly to the table: picks up the phone: McGaf-
ferty begins again to pace the room behind him.*

IMMELMAN (*in the phone*)

                                        Davis.
Yes... I'll hold on... hurry it...

McGAFFERTY

                                        Who told them?
Who cut the black queen from the shuffled pack?

Who flipped the two-bit token tails up telling?
Christ! we'll teach them how the future's told!

IMMELMAN (*in the phone*)
... Deposit in Omaha crediting Indianapolis...

McGAFFERTY
After so long so dark are they so certain?
How do they know so surely the day's come?
Who told them so?

*The door opens to half admit Ione: she is a woman of thirty:
handsome: full-blooded: exuberant: too well dressed: her mouth too
red: a vivid quality of life and intelligence in her face and move-
ments. McGafferty turns: sees her. She looks at Immelman, the
phone still to his mouth.*

IONE (*a half whisper*)
Hello! I'll be outside.

McGAFFERTY
No: no. Come in.

IMMELMAN (*in the phone*)
... Advise Detroit by wire:
Call me back.

Immelman puts the receiver down: looks at Ione.

McGAFFERTY (*to Ione*)

You've met the...

IONE

Guess we've bowed.

How are you?

IMMELMAN (*stiffly*)

Yes. How are you?

IONE (*too sweetly*)

How are *you*?

Immelman looks from McGafferty to the ticker and back.

IMMELMAN

Well — I'll be going.

IONE

Don't be going. I'll go.

She drops into one of the large chairs facing the audience: her back to the two men and the room. Immelman crosses to the door.

IMMELMAN

I'll be going. Plenty left to do.

54

He starts to go: turns at the door.

About the — won't you give the orders?

MᶜGAFFERTY

Orders?

Immelman looks at the back of Ione's head.

IMMELMAN

Thing I spoke of.

IONE

He has secrets too.

MᶜGAFFERTY

What orders? Give what orders?

IMMELMAN

On the loans.

MᶜGAFFERTY

What orders on the loans? Speak up man!

IMMELMAN

Call them.

55

McGAFFERTY

Why should we call them? Look here: what's behind it?
What's the sudden mystery? Why should we?
What's been eating at you?

IMMELMAN

Well — precaution.
Precautionary measure. Can't be sure...

Immelman gestures toward the ticker. McGafferty turns and looks at him intently. There is a too-long silence: the sound of the ticker across it threatening: insistent.

IMMELMAN *(uneasily)*

Perhaps I'd better... If I may... There's something...
Sooner or later...

He looks again at Ione and away.

IONE

Don't mind me. I'm listening.

McGafferty suddenly turns: walks across to the table: he speaks briskly and cheerfully, first to Ione, then to Immelman.

McGAFFERTY

Good Lord! It's after seven. Well Ione? —
We'll decide it. — Hungrier this evening? —
Get the figures. We'll decide it. — Ready? —

56

IMMELMAN

Perhaps I'd better tell you first...

McGAFFERTY (*not looking at him*)
Tomorrow.
There'll be time enough. We'll talk tomorrow.
Ready Ione?

Immelman opens the door: Ione turns in her chair.

IONE

Must you? Then good-night!
Good-night! Good-night!

Immelman looks again at McGafferty and goes out. Ione leans back in her chair. McGafferty begins to pace the room. The lights fade out: the light comes on in The Street. *A crowd stands there.*

A MAN (*reading*)
Crisis   increasing: crash
Grows

CONFUSED VOICES (*in increasing tempo*)
Crash... crisis...

Crash crisis increasing...

Crisis increasing...

Crash

57

Crisis increasing...

Crisis...

A WOMAN

Neither the last nor the least of
God's creatures escapes from it —
Smashed with the stone — the nape
Broken — legs bashed.

A MAN (*reading*)

Cash   exhausted

Last

Credits   exhausted

CONFUSED VOICES

Last

Cash credits exhausted...

A WOMAN

Last hope lost.

A WOMAN

Last hope and the first too.

A MAN

The days of our lives were rehearsed by
Long-dead men in our places

58

Facing the sun — facing the
Same stars. The signs are
Not changed: they remind us.

A Man

Others before us have feared it in
Night's silence — hearing the
Always nearer and ceaseless
Sound as in winter trees where the
Wind comes: the hush and the
Unseen violent rushing: the
Night silent awaiting it:
Click of the latch at the gate:
Scud on the tree-caught star.

A Woman

Farther than sleep — farther than
Sleep remembers — elder than
Oldest sleep — have beheld
Giant figures shadowing
Evening with fatal hands.
The dark shapes return to us.
The old ones: doomers of earth:
Namers of death: foresayers of
Men's fortune and fate in the
World's way have returned to us.

A Woman

Fear and by night returns to us.

59

A Man

No chance disaster
Darkens as this does — casting
Sure and deliberate shadow of
Death before it — adding to
Ruin ruin patiently.

A Woman

Many in sorrow's nation —
Dead kings and the trembling
Speakers of silence — remember them.

A Man

Long since have discerned
Unseen currents turning the
Life back and to windward:
Beating the strongest in:
Defeating the best: cancelling
Labor to every man — his
Hands torn with the toil and the
Toil useless: spoiling
Even highest hopes: the
Finest blinded and groping.

A Man

An unknown power opposes us.
Perverse rivers flow from the
Past forward altering

Seaways — flooding salt in the
Fresh streams — drowning
Meadows of richest ground —
Carrying under even the
Oldest dykes — leaving the
Roads gone: the bridges
Washed out by the ditch —
The orchards choked in the shingle.

A MAN

None may withstand it. The single and
Stubborn arm against mystery
Falls and the raised fist will
Fall: the opening fingers.

A MAN

Neither may strongest men by
Great wealth nor with power of
Will nor of force defend us —
They also now —
By time's flooding river
Swollen with ancient storms in the
Upland years before us are
Borne down — delivered to
Sudden and terrible swiftness of
Turbulent waters lifting the
Ancientest trees: drowning
Cities on holy ground.

61

The light fades out in the Street. It comes on again in McGaf-
ferty's Office. Ione sits in the deep chair still. McGafferty still
paces the room. There is a moment's silence: even the ticker silent.

IONE (*yawning*)
I said good-night! I said...
Cripes but I'm sunk: down: sunk: scuttled —

She yawns again.

I thought you'd never come. So I came. Waited
Hours! Hours and hours and hours and hours.

She yawns.

Pink's a hell of a color to wait in — a pink
Room! A pretty pink room! A pretty
Pink girl in a pink room! A pink
Punk. Pink punk paces apartment.
Even the dog's pink: pinkish: punkish: the
Punk Peke. O to Hell with it! Pink!
The years I've waited in pink for five-thirty!

She lies back for a moment with her eyes closed: her body volup-
tuous in the deep chair.

You know something? Pink smells. There's an odor.
Well if you don't believe me try it yourself.
Smells different by candle-light.

62

She opens her eyes: half turns her head.

God you're responsive!

*McGafferty continues to walk up and down in the room. She settles
back.*

Night! I said good-night: good-night: good-night!...
'For her gait if she be walking...' Gait!
A horse gaits: a woman moves like a panther: it's
Beautiful! 'Be she sitting I desire her
For her state's sake.' Listen! 'And admire her
For her wit if she be talking.' Have I been
Talking? Or how long? Sitting too! In state like a
Dead Emperor: Empress: Empire! Take thine
Empire Caesar that subjected lies
Prey to thy ravishes...

She opens her eyes: turns: looks at McGafferty.

Strange feeling — alone in an
Empty city: echo answering echo:
Dancing your pretty feet off and who cares?

McGAFFERTY

Forgive me: I'm dull I know: difficult day:
Worst day I guess I can remember.
Maybe I'm getting old.

63

*He leans over the back of Ione's chair and kisses her mechanically:
straightens as the ticker begins again: crosses to it, picking up the
tape.*

IONE

Sure! Like oak —

The better for it. Darling! —

And what happened?

The old ram butt you? God what a bleating bore!

McGAFFERTY

O Immelman's all right. It's me. I'm done for.
Haven't you heard? Dead.

IONE

Nobody tells me.

Nobody tells me anything. Millions of people
All keeping the news from me — buying the newspapers.
Do you think they should? You tell me darling.
When did you learn?

McGAFFERTY

Today. A fortune teller.

No cards. No tricks. Nothing.

IONE

A fortune teller! Mr. McGafferty went to a —
Well for the love of God!

64

MCGAFFERTY

Went? No:

No! He came to me — parcel of Radicals.

IONE

Oh! Radicals! What did the Radicals say? I
Love Radicals! Pretty pretty people!
What did the Radicals say to you darling?

MCGAFFERTY

Done for.

Dead and done for. My time's done. I'm finished.
Destiny's got me. History's through with me. Fate's
Fed up with the likes of my lot. Myself — there's
Blood on my head already!

IONE

Ah! They've looked.

Darling they've been looking.

MCGAFFERTY

All this row —

Banks closing like bars — it's the devil come after us.
End of a world: end of a man: end of
Everything! Washed up! Done for! The end of it!

IONE

It's beautiful darling! Don't you think it's beautiful?
Mr. McGafferty's done for! Isn't it beautiful?

65

Could I have a touch of Scotch? You know I'm
Sad to think you're done for!

*McGafferty takes a decanter from a small table: pours a drink into
a glass.*

McGAFFERTY

Beautiful? No!
Beautiful's not the word I think I'd use.
Ever have a blind man lay his fingers
Smooth as a cicatrice across your face and
Feel a film of blood between?

Ione leans back in her chair: the glass in her hand.

IONE

No darling!
Blind men never touch me. Poor poor done for!
Poor dead and done for! It's a kind of dirge —

*She declaims theatrically. The ticker beats in counter rhythm under
the sound of her voice.*

All dead and done for
Let him be laid
Whose race is run:
Whom grave is made for.
No pretty ladye
Him to persuade:

66

No heat of sun for
His limbs ever:
Who's taken to his bride the spade:
Earth for his cover.

She drinks from the glass.

It's a pretty thing.

McGAFFERTY

You make it pretty.
You'd make the promise of a child's death pretty.
Lightness like yours is like the beetle's back:
Brittle. It gilds and gleams to any color.

IONE (*deep in the chair: the glass at her mouth*)
Lightness? Lightness you say? You call it lightness?
Lightly as tears that barely touch the cheek
But let the blood stop! It's the woman's courage
Wearing the sleeve upon the heart that fools you —
Wearing the bright sleeve on the broken heart.

She drinks.

Women are wonderful in tears I think — or
Don't you? There was one day — afternoon —
Toulon it was: the sea beyond the shutters...

67

McGafferty

What is there that could touch you!

Ione

O I weep
Easily: evenings and every night: for nothing.

McGafferty

I think you'd take it laughing if I told you
Even the worst they promised me had come.

Ione

How should I take it? Sobbing? With my eyes full?
You with your name in metal on the doors!
I'll cry but not for fairy stories: not for
Bad dreams either. No. How should I take it?

McGafferty

Why laughing! Laughing! It's a thing to laugh at.
What hurt would you feel if the words were true?
What grief would touch you if the time's against me —
The chance gone wrong: the turn of the earth unkind?
What pain would touch your heart? Old men are laughable.
Old men's ills are laughable. Old men's loves are
Always to be laughed at.

Ione

Love does he say?

At love?...

68

She rises slowly: the glass still in her hand.

Have we not given love and taken it?
What *did* we give and take then? What's the thing
Given and taken in a bed at night but
Love? What other have you ever wanted?
And if that's love why where's the laughter then?
Am I the cheap and purchasable whore who
Gives her willingness but not her will?
I never gave my mouth yet but the fame and
Wonder made me: least of all to you.
I only give my mouth where it can praise.

MCGAFFERTY

And when the praise is gone you'll cease to give it.

IONE

Oh I'm a shrewder whore than you would think.
I choose the fame that lasts. When your fame goes
There'll be no breath nor mouth to give or lend to
Anyone. It never will.

The whirring of the ticker fills the room.

MCGAFFERTY
You think not?
Listen!

69

The beat of the ticker begins: pulse-like and mechanical.

That clock counts its time by changes.
Some men say they've seen the shadowy figures
Shift already on the darkened dial.
I have not seen them yet — but I may see them.

He breaks off: walks distractedly in the room.

Deeds are the brittle keepers. Our time's fame is
Reef coral: dead ones erected it: life
Sucks at the edge with the salt bitterness: seas over-
Whelm it!

He turns violently upon her.

You who need the weight of fame to
Feel an old man's body on your body —
What will you do when the fame is gone?

IONE *(bitterly)*
There'll be the man still...

McGAFFERTY
And you'll take the man?

IONE
Why not? Why shouldn't I? I've taken him.

70

McGafferty

You've taken him! You've taken what? You think the
Greatness of a man's at least a man?
Yes. Or a man at last is only greatness: an
Empty shoe and the foot gone from it: vacant: the
Shape a woman makes of him to love:
Named and the face gone: kept as girls keep favors:
Fragile and flimsy as the brittle ash that
Once was water-leaves but lines a book now:
Crumbled as easily as that. You'll find the
Scurf of greatness underneath your nails and
Think with loathing of the man who touched you.

Ione

No... not loathing. Look at me. I tell you
Look!

It is not like you to have said so:
No — nor not like me to hear you say so:
Not like either of us to have heard or
Said.

McGafferty

Like what then? Like the aging man
Stripped to the twitching withers of his age and
Begging pity of the girl he forced once?
Lovely as that? So lovely? A sweet sight!
Not to be looked at!

71

IONE

>   Oh!...

*Ione drops to the arm of the deep chair: her head against the back:
her eyes closed. The sound of the ticker is louder: the beat more
rapid. McGafferty moves toward it: stands.*

McGAFFERTY

>   Christ! Will it stop now?

Hours it should have stopped!...

>   But no! Not pity!

Pity and your kind of love would breed like
Stoat and rabbit! Pity turns contempt when
What's now pitiful was great once and the pride
Wore it for admiration!...

>   Hours it should have!

Ticking as clocks do! But not time — disaster!
Disaster ticking from a clockwork box!
God! If you listen long enough you think the
Clockwork makes the harm come — woundup clockwork
Clicking the luck out like the nickel candy
Coined from a trick machine!...

>   What is it you want of me?

I can lose so easily what you want!...

72

Disaster after disaster after disaster!
Drumming disasters out with the count of the clock!
Clicking them out of the clockwork clean on a ribbon and
No stopping it! Wound up and no stopping it!
Grinding them out and no stopping it!...

Sweet sight!
A sweet sight in any country! Horrible!...

McGafferty touches the ticker.

God! Will the thing stop! Is the groping world
Mechanical and grinds on like a gear-nest —
Ignorant in the sullen oil — that drives the
Wheels toward nothing — anything — nothing — death — but
Drives them! Drives them! Drives them! Always drives them!

*The lights begin to fade out. McGafferty picks up the tape: reads it:
tears it from the machine wildly.*

MCGAFFERTY

Jesus Christ!

IONE

What is it? Tell me!

MCGAFFERTY

Michigan.
Moratorium. All banks closed tomorrow...

73

The lights go.

Moratorium!...

The lights come on in The Street.   *A great crowd stands there.*

CONFUSED VOICES

Moratorium...

Wait!

Moratorium...

Wait!

Wait!

Moratorium!

Wait!

What does it mean?

What is it for?

Wait!

74

What can they do to us more than the
Cold's done?...

                        The four
Years?

                What is there more of it?

What is there more than the haste of the
Wind's heel in the door they can
Do to us?

                Wait! Wait!

A WOMAN

Ah the bastards! the big ones! the
Kings of the world! And the worst of it
Here on our backs: and deserting us!

A MAN

What have they done to us: lenders of
Hunger to living men:
Hoarders of life: McGafferty...

A MAN

Surely our Rod and our Staff and our
Help in the world! And they'd keep us the

Hunger and cold and the sleepless and
Wet nights from our skin if we'd
Give them the cash for their winnings and
Give them the work of our hands and
Give them the coal and the land and be
Silent with awe and amazed at the
Cities they built us and praising them.

A MAN

Christ let them go! Let them rot in the
Thunder of sunlight forgotten!

A MAN

Let them be lost in the leap of the
Landward seas and the sweeping of
Wind through the shallow flowers!

A MAN

The world's to the nameless now.

A WOMAN

The world's to the unnamed man with the
Reckless speech who will stand to the
Cold marching of stars and
Shriek in the face of it hardening
Man's mortal body to
Bear and endure like a god: to
Live in the running of time like the
Trout in the stream climbing it!

A WOMAN

The world's to the nameless man who'll
Brag in the sun and withstand it and
Stiffen our hearts that drift like
Fog on a wave's lifting
Following every current!

A WOMAN

Theirs is the world who will stand to the
Circle of anguish opposing it:
Giving us — drifting ghosts — a
Man's weight that the mark of our
Shoes may live after us: sharpening
Odor of air to our tongues
Till the hunger of hope is among us.

The light fades out in the Street: comes on in McGafferty's Office.
McGafferty sits at the table, Ione leaning over him.

IONE

No but come with me. I've made a fire:
Four logs and a pitch-pine knot. We'll see the
Shadows after softly on the ceiling.

She leans against his shoulder.

Once the sunlight from the sea made shadows.
I remember how the shutters blurred and

Blinded toward the sea. It smelled of water.
Darkness wakened us from so much sun.
I think all night the gulls cried on the water.
Come! Please come with me.

McGAFFERTY (*his face in his hands*)
Christ! there were banks
Broke before this and the sun rose...

IONE
Won't you come?
The room is far-off night times and the street cars
Infinite under you the way the surf
Sounds on the sea-reef in those islands.

McGAFFERTY
There were panics —
Actual panics — smash after smash — rich men
Poor in a night and rich again. We've forgotten.
Men forget...

He said that!...

Men forget...
Yes but help too they forget. The hardship
Dries out like a drowned man's shape in sand and
Children lie there at the sea's edge. Worse and
More than worse we've stood and we've forgotten.
78

IONE

Yes! We've all forgotten. We'll forget.

McGAFFERTY (*rising*)

Gawking as girls would at a waking scarecrow!
Watching a shifting shadow like a hen that
Sees the hawk shape circle on the grass! To
Hell with it! To Hell with cries and courage
Facing the darkness on an empty stair!
I'll close the door! With you I will!

He takes her in his arms.

IONE

                                    I thought you
Hated me the way you watched me.

McGAFFERTY

                                    Hated!
Maybe it is hate when the aching skin
Crawls at the thought of you: the belly knots with
Anguish at the thought of you: the nails
Tear at the palms — the teeth tear at the tongue with
Thought of you. Hate! The kind of hate
Condemned men have for food that if they lack they'll
Starve for it: or if they have it — starve!

IONE

Nothing has changed then. Nothing real has changed.

79

She leads him toward the door.

McGAFFERTY

Only forgetfulness! Only forgetting! Only the
Trick time plays us with his side-show mirrors
Twisting the thing to come until it's vast:
Larger than life: grotesque: unhuman: threatening —
Glozing the thing behind until the small
Familiar image glimmers like a hearth: the
Hurt all out of it: the harm gone: charming —
And yet the two are one thing: our own selves:
Our own shapes twice repeated: once behind us:
Once before us in the left-hand glass!

The telephone rings.

Fear is the face we turn to what's before us:
Fear is the face reflected back: our own but
Terrifying!

The telephone rings.

IONE

No! We must go! Please go!
Please! We can't wait! I can't wait! There's something
Dangerous in this room — I don't know —

80

McGafferty picks up the telephone as it rings again. He is looking at Ione as he speaks mechanically into the instrument.

McGAFFERTY (*in the phone*)

Yes.

IONE

Don't you believe me when I say I must? I
Must go — must go —

McGAFFERTY (*in the phone*)

No. Not now.

IONE

Oh hurry!

McGAFFERTY (*in the phone*)

Any time tomorrow.

IONE

Please! Oh please!

McGAFFERTY (*in the phone*)

Shelton? What did? Who did?

Ione drops her hand from the door-knob at the change in his voice.

IONE

Oh...

81

McGafferty (*in the phone*)

Well, ask him!...

Never mind that! Ask him!...

Ione goes back to the chair: stands beside it.

Ione

They won't let you.

They won't let you come. I knew they wouldn't.
No. I knew they wouldn't let you.

McGafferty (*in the phone*)

All right!

Send him up. I'll wait here.

(*to Ione*)

Griggs. Of American.

Something's happened to Shelton. You know Shelton.
Ran the company fifteen years. The best of them.
Griggs is an ass — a lawyer — a damn fool.

Ione does not reply. She drops again into the deep chair. There is a silence — the ticker loud in it.

McGafferty (*stiffly*)

Sorry to keep you.

82

IONE

No. It doesn't matter.
It's nothing. It's the purest folly. Like the
Fear a child has in the attic room where
Someone died a long time back — as though he
Still must do it. As though walls foretold
Things that already'd happened. Or remembered
Things not happened yet that must though. Oh I
Am a child you see. It's not a bad room.
We'll light a candle in it. Candles for courage.
The things we see we fear less.

McGAFFERTY

Fear! Fear what?
I tell you there's not anything to fear!
It's natural. A year from now we'll laugh and
Wonder how we talked so. Like the moon
The time itself has dark and shining quarters.
The time turns as the moon turns — bright though dark:
You'll see the light again.

The door opens silently. Griggs enters and advances into the circle
of light. He is a thin, dry, harsh-faced man in late middle-age.
Ione, facing away from the door, does not see him. There is a
moment's silence. Then McGafferty at the desk raises his head.

McGAFFERTY

Is that you Griggs?

83

GRIGGS

Am I intruding?

McGAFFERTY

Sit down.

GRIGGS

What I have to...

McGAFFERTY

Anything you want to say you can.

GRIGGS

What I have to say is serious.

IONE

Shall I? —

McGAFFERTY

No. Stay here. Go on Griggs.

GRIGGS (*shrugging*)

Shelton's **dead.**

McGAFFERTY (*rising*)

Shelton's...

84

GRIGGS

Dead. He shot himself. They called me.

McGAFFERTY

It's not true!

GRIGGS

It's true enough. I saw him.

McGAFFERTY

No! Not true! It can't be! Let the rest
Rot with this creeping fear — not that man! Shelton! — the
Bull's face and the hands like fists — it can't! He'd
Crack the ceiling laughing at you. Try it!
Tell *him* the break's against him! Tell him that!
He'd laugh until he choked. He'd cough with laughter.
Men like that don't kill themselves!

GRIGGS

I know.

*McGafferty drops slowly back into his chair: the violence drained
out of him.*

McGAFFERTY

And yet... he did. How did he?

85

GRIGGS

How? I've told you.

Forty-four in the mouth. Look here McGafferty —
Let's omit the appropriate speeches and sentiments.
We've made you chairman.

McGAFFERTY

Where?

GRIGGS

Where what?... The washroom.

For God's sake listen to me! Will you take it?
You said you never would — I know! There's no choice.
News leaks out like beer at a broken bung.
The banks are breaking now. This kills them. Will you?
Only your name can stop it.

McGAFFERTY

Even Shelton!

Dead in a urinal — the grey-haired man —
Greasy blood on the mopped marble — respectable —
His father's seal on his watch-chain — shoes polished —
Dressed decently — not for that though —

GRIGGS

Will you?

Will you McGafferty?

86

MCGAFFERTY

What did he see do you think?
What did he see on the ground glass of the door — the
Light behind it? — see or think he saw there?
Something not to run from: not to meet.
Something inescapable enough to
Jerk the gun hand.

GRIGGS

How should I know!

MCGAFFERTY

I know!
Dressed — not ready — not in his bed either —
The light bulb staring at the staring eyes —
Dressed decently but not for that! I know.
He knew them also. He knew who they were.
Give them time their hand will always show.
They'll pile it on too thick until we know them:
Heap it higher than a man could: crowd us:
Cross us in purposes that no man knows:
Follow us longer than a man would follow! —
O we know the signs by now — the adversities
Pure and causeless and crank as a child's murder:
The punishments not for evil: wrongs rewarded:
The will not like our will but like a will:
The law that's not our law but that compels us...

87

GRIGGS

For God's sake listen to me man!

MCGAFFERTY

I hear you!
I hear them too! He heard them! Room to room
To that last shameful white-tiled empty room! —
By whom? He never saw them but he knew.
The camphor taste of fear: the silence following:
Sucking the gun's end: cold help: sleepy nipple:
Metal to nurse him quiet with —

GRIGGS

McGafferty —
Listen McGafferty! Listen! There's no time!
I tell you there's no time! Another hour —
Less — a moment — who knows — even now...
I say you've got to. Listen man. You've got to.

MCGAFFERTY

Time! You think there's ever time to trick them?
They keep the time too!

GRIGGS

God you have no choice!

88

McGafferty

No! Nor you! Nor anyone! We choose
But not by alternates: by one — then one.
We play the breaks and get them or don't get them.

Griggs

You won't?

McGafferty

It's past our hands.

Griggs

That from McGafferty!
That from you! You're sick! You're seeing things! The
Drinks have got you.

McGafferty

Yes. You think they're shadows!
You think this creeping ruin is a shadow!
You think it's chance the banks go one by one
Closing the veins as cold does — killing secretly —
Freezing the heart — ruin following ruin —
The country dying of it — towns dead — land dead —
Hunger limping every road — you think it's
Chance that does it? You think! So did I!
I do not think so now. I think they wish it.
We cannot see them but they're there: they loom
Behind the seen side like the wind in curtains.

89

GRIGGS

O for the love of —

*Griggs turns abruptly away toward the door: swings back into the
circle of light.*

GRIGGS

Think of the record McGafferty!
They keep the record even in times like these.
Everything else wipes out but there's the record:
A man appeals upon the naked record:
They won't look past the record. Fifty years and
Where will you stand? Even kids will judge you! —
Could have saved the show and wouldn't!

MCGAFFERTY

Could have!
Could have you think?

GRIGGS

By nodding once! By saying
Yes — once!

MCGAFFERTY

You're wrong then. No one could have.
Nothing to come was ever changed beforehand.
It came. It's coming now.

GRIGGS

What's coming? What is?
Nothing that can't be mended: nothing new.

90

Trouble's no unexpected guest in these parts.
The new thing's not the trouble man. It's you. It's
Your kind waiting for the great disaster: —
Standing as steers would to the butcher's maul: your
Heads down: ears back: eyes shut: dumb: — a man would
Almost say you wanted it — to watch you.

The ticker begins violently. McGafferty turns sharply toward it.

God McGafferty... I think you do!
I think by God you do! I think you want it!
Look at your eyes now! Look! You've turned us in! You've
Checked out: chucked us: let the chance go! No — it's
True! You want it. And you've let it come! You've
Quit McGafferty! You've quit! You hear me?
Quit! May God in Heaven pay you!

Griggs goes out.

IONE (*standing by her chair*)
No!
It's not true. It's not true. I...

McGafferty turns toward her. She sees his face. Suddenly, impulsively, she crosses to him.

IONE
Nothing matters.
Nothing matters any more but us.

91

I was a fool. I didn't understand. I
Hurt you.

There is a pause: McGafferty staring at her.

McGAFFERTY

Now you understand?

IONE

I do.

McGAFFERTY

What do you?

IONE

That you're fagged out.

McGAFFERTY

Licked?

IONE

I love you!

O my dear I love you!

McGAFFERTY

Yes! You love me!
Licked. The old man's licked. And still she loves him.

92

IONE

Is it so strange? Is that so strange to you?
Have I no right to say so? Old? — Are you old?
I do not know if you are old. I know I
Love you. Is it strange that I should love you?
Is it unnatural in me? — perverse? — shameful?
Must I be sorry for it?

McGAFFERTY (*rising*)

No. It's generous —
Honorable in you — kind. Take to your bed a
Great man's name and lose it and still keep the
Bed place empty for the man! It's generous!
What will you use now nights as other women
Borrow a lover's face to hide a husband's
Bearing a weight they don't bear? What will help you —
Now the greatness is all gone? — the fame gone?

IONE

Nothing's gone. You must not say so.

McGAFFERTY

No —
It robs your pity of the chance!

IONE

My pity!
I to pity you! I love you! Is there nothing

93

Simple enough — not even love — to be given
Once and for all in your world like a small coin and
Never asked for again?

McGafferty

Given in charity!
Given and taken! The usages of failure! To be
Fooled: and know you're fooled and yet to play you're
Not fooled! So that kindness still may fool you!
Play that you're deaf because they say you're deaf to
Hide your doting! Play you're loved because the
Jig's up... and the love's a comfort... to the giver of it!
No. You keep your gifts for those that beg them.
Love that can be given or not given —
Love like that's not love but gift and says so —
Pity's proof: the final verdict: sentence!...
Love for the loser!

McGafferty moves violently across the room.

Love!

He turns upon her.

You think I've lost?
You think you know what Immelman would tell me?
You think the thing he had to tell was that?
You heard him and you think he would have said so?
Well we'll learn!

94

He picks up the phone. The street crowd is seen gathering. More and more numerous it surrounds the office as the scene proceeds.

You think I fear to learn?

IONE (*slowly moving toward the door*)

No...

Nor anything...

I do not know you.

McGAFFERTY (*in the phone*)
Get me Immelman.... Well get him!   Get him!

IONE (*she speaks half to herself*)
Something in your face now is not yours but
Hateful of you: like the luckless look that
Makes the dying dangerous and strange.

McGAFFERTY (*in the phone*)
Is that you Immelman? You wished to tell me...
No! the phone will do. Go on...

I hear you...

Yes...

95

Yes...

Yes...

There is a silence: not even the ticker. The street crowd draws nearer.
Then McGafferty's voice: changed: flat.

Yes. I'm here still....
No...

I know...

It happens...

Well — it's happened.

No: not your fault: no one's: no one did it.
No one could have helped it. We're like sheep
Shut in a runway and one turn to take: we're
Walled in like a cornered hunted cat our
Least move watched for: our last lunge of will
Checked at the gesture...

Nothing. No. Forget it!
Nothing that you needed hear. No matter.
Well we'll think... we'll see...

Yes. Tell them. Tell them.
Call the Times and tell them...

96

Frozen loans:

Closed: you tell them...

Yes but later. Call me...

He puts the receiver down: turns to Ione — she by the door now.

MᴄGᴀꜰꜰᴇʀᴛʏ

Christ! Must they knock us down with black-jacks — wring
    us with
Midnight questions — twist our thumbs to make us
Say we see them?

Iᴏɴᴇ

Listen to me! Listen!

MᴄGᴀꜰꜰᴇʀᴛʏ

O we'll talk! We'll talk! They'll make us talk!
They'll force the truth! — is that it? They'll be tough!
They'll get the truth out publicly with witnesses!
They'll force us will they? We'll confess it all?
We'll say that fate's our master and confess it?
We'll bear them witness? Well there's one that won't!
By God there's one that won't — the grinning gangster —
Teeth through the tongue and silence and refuse!
Insolent and refusing!

97

IONE

Luckless! Luckless!

McGAFFERTY

Let them be certain of it! Let them brag!
There's one they'll never break to say they broke him!
One that holds his tongue — the wilful mask to
Mock them as it always mocked them!

IONE

O! what

Curse is on you!

*She drops her hands to her sides: goes out: the door closing behind
her. The lights fade: McGafferty swings violently back toward the
table.*

McGAFFERTY

God there's one that won't!

*The lights go out. The ticker, sounding more and more slowly in
the silence, becomes almost inaudible: a vibration of air. Then abruptly, in the same rhythm, the flashes of the bulletin strike into the
crowd now thick in* The Street.

VOICES (*breathlessly*)

Who is it

Dead?

98

Who does it say?

Who — is it he?

          Is it suicide?

Who is it?

        Dead! — McGafferty's
Dead!

      It's him — it's McGafferty —
Dead!

      He's dead!

          McGafferty's
Dead!

      A Woman
    It's the end of them — quit of them!

  An Old Woman (*exultantly*)
Bellies bitter with drinking the
Weak tears do you fear the
Fall of the walls and the sky
High over you shining there?

       99

A MAN (*exultantly*)

Mouths bitter with hate and the
Aching of tears have you tasted the
New water that springs in the
Hollow of thirst in your fingers?

A MAN (*exultantly*)

Eyes blind with the sleet and the
Freezing of night have you seen how the
Wind's in the rising East and the
Mountains of morning increasing?

A WOMAN

The roof's fallen! The sun
Stands on the sky with his wonder.

A WOMAN

The wind — the wind's in the house!

A WOMAN

The walls open arousing us!

A MAN

Wildly as swollen river the
Dark will of the world
Flooded on rock rushes
Raving — bearing the brush down:

100

Breaking from ancient banks.
Cities are buried. The man
Drowns in his door who opposes it.

VOICES

Follow!

Give!

Go with the
Rushing of time in us!

Make of the
Silence of fate a trumpet!
Make of the time a drum!

March!

Shout!

A MAN

Run with the
Marching men: with the thunder of
Thousand heels on the earth —
Making of mortal burden a
Banner to shout and to break in the
Blazing of sunlight and shaken there!

101

VOICES

Take it!

Be taken!

The trumpet of
Time in our ears and the brazen and
Breaking shout of our days!

MANY VOICES

Man's fate is a drum!